ISBN 978-1-332-87934-2
PIBN 10302999

1 MONTH OF
FREE
READING

at

www.ForgottenBooks.com

By purchasing this book you are eligible for one month membership to ForgottenBooks.com, giving you unlimited access to our entire collection of over 700,000 titles via our web site and mobile apps.

To claim your free month visit:

www.forgottenbooks.com/free302999

Sunday Law, Liberty and License.

A Discourse before the Sinai Congregation,

December 16th, 1888,

BY E. G. HIRSCH.

Experience is the great task-master of mankind.   In the merciless school of sin, suffering and failure, man learns to know the eternal laws of his own being.   That knowledge comes to him not at once ; it flashes not upon him with the full glory of the noon hour, only gradually does its splendor unfold itself to him.   Truth is a sun that has its hours of rising and of setting, its eclipses and its clouds. Slowly as the king of day scales the heaven's heights, and contends against the shadows and the mists, does truth ascend the golden steps toward the zenith, and vigorously has it to war against jealous obstacles. Through the mazes of error man is led to the majesty of truth; and what we call experience is but the remembrance of the road traveled o'er, is the record of attempts that failed, of battles waged with doubtful result, of victories finally accomplished.   When experience hath spoken, experience well established and securely grounded, theory, airy and assumed, must lay the finger of silence on the glib lips. The time for speculation is o'er, when from the fields of actual life are brought home the rich sheaves or the ripe fruits.

Experience now gives proof that the weekly interruption of labor through the day of rest, corresponds to a deeply rooted want of human nature, and is thus a necessity and an invaluable blessing. Popular prejudice largely believes that only the religious-minded can plead for the observation of the Sabbath day. It is, according to this opinion, an institution of the church. Those that have weaned themselves of priest and preacher need not shape their life in accordance with the old ecclesiastical prescriptions. Whether the Sabbath originally was, or was not a religious institution I must for the moment keep in abeyance; but there can be no doubt on this point that a day of rest is indispensable to the welfare of individual and of society at large. None will suspect in the writings of the socialist Proudhon a religious bias, or accuse him of sectarian narrowness and theological fanaticism. Still in his booklet on the celebration of Sunday ("De la celebration du Dimanche"), he comes to the conclusion just worded by me, through considerations of a purely economic and moral kind. Other men, and not alone of the favored classes, but also from among the working people, have expressed themselves to the same effect. For many years past the Swiss societies for the promotion of public welfare have been busy with this very question. They have offered premiums for the best solution; they have by speech and by pen agitated for a more general observation of the weekly day of rest. Nor is Germany indifferent, as is generally assumed, on this subject. Government and private associations are gathering statistics on the extent of Sunday labor, and on its effects upon the moral and material prosperity of the people. Dignitaries of the state, generals, authors, professors, leaders of workingmen, conservatists, socialists, all are raising their voice to insure a more general cessation from labor of any kind throughout the German empire, and are pleading for a more quiet and dignified manner of spending the day. In brief, Proudhon is right when he says Sunday rest is not a subject of opinion, but is founded on actual knowledge. It is a well established fact, that even beasts and dead machines are stronger and wear out less speedily, if allowed to share in the periodical rest of the Sabbath. In the books I find a practical example of this in a story about two men, carriers of goods from one place in the east of Germany to another in the west, before the days of our railroads. To cover the distance between the two points, eight to ten weeks were consumed. One of the two was in the habit of allowing his horses and his vehicle to rest over Sunday, while the other, grumbling at the unnecessary delay, took the whim in one of their expeditions to push on regardless of the day of rest. In this wise he expected to outstrip his competitor by at least seven days. The companion was satisfied, and made the wager that, notwithstanding his stopping over every seventh day, he would be the first to reach the end of the journey. The wager was accepted, and the result showed that the observer of the Sabbath was the more prudent of the two men, for actually he reached his destination one week ahead of the other; and besides his horses and wagon were in good condition, while the other arrived with wagon ruined, and with horses over-tired, over-worked and jaded. This story is not taken from a Sunday-school tract, but I found it in a little book written by a physician, named Niemeyer, who, leaving religious considerations out of the scope of his inquiry, pleads strongly for the observation of the weekly day of rest from the standpoint of hygiene. Experience further seems to have taught that the interruption of labor should follow regularly on the seventh pay after six days of work. The French revolution, in its desire to turn everything topsy-turvy, abolished, as you well know, the weekly Sabbath, and substituted for it the decade; that is, a day of festivities occurring every ten days—three in one month. We have the testimony of a working man, who during this time lived in Paris, that the new arrangement by no means conferred the benefits of the old. Whether or not the number seven corresponds to a physiological law as Cabanis, philosopher and physician both, claims, who maintains that the fluctuations of our body's temperature run in cycles of seven days, is not for me to say, but I may be allowed to quote again the words of Proudhon: "Shorten the week by one day and the want of rest is not yet pressing, but lengthen the week by one day and you have over-fatigue. Set aside every three days half a day for rest, and you have want of symmetry and plan. Assign after twelve days of work two days of rest, and you will ruin the working man with leisure, after having first exhausted him with labor." In truth, the best lovers of the people are agreed that one day in seven is the best arrangement, and experience bolsters this agreement.

But how should this day of rest be celebrated? It may not be superfluous in this connection to cast a glance, hasty and sketchy at the history of the Sabbath, as far as we can trace it. I quarrel not with those simple believers for whom questions of this kind are answered in the biblical record. I do not desire to disturb their assurance that the Sabbath was instituted by God himself. The opening chapter of Genesis is indeed a stirring poem. The thought that after the completion of the world, God affixed to it his seal of approval by the sign of the Sabbath is strong and uplifting. That thought remains true, whether we read the signs of the heavens according to a new key, or still decipher the inscriptions of the vault above according to the dialect of the fathers. The critical school is deeply conscious of the moral truths crystallized in the old legends. It can spare the husk, but in breaking it, sets free what is fundamental. The Sabbath *is* a seal of perfection, a witness to self approval of work done; and it remains so whether we locate its source in the lands of earth or lift it up into the regions of the heavens. To my mind there is no doubt that the Sabbath was originally linked to the worship of the moon, and was an institution of the Shemites in those removed times even before the Hebrew had differentiated himself from his kinsmen. A number of competent scholars have found proof of the observation of a day somewhat like to the Sabbath among the Assyrians. Other scholars are disinclined to allow this construction of the tablets bearing on the point. No matter whether we follow one party or the other in this controversy, it is plain that the biblical record gives sufficient hint to suggest that the Sabbath was in some form or other among the institutions of the Hebrews before the Sinaitic period. In Amos, in Isaiah, and in other passages of the prophets, Sabbath and new moon are quoted in one breath. But little observation was necessary to teach that the moon consumed twenty-eight solar days in her fickle passage across the nightly sky, and that every seventh day apparently she came to a point of rest. Hence the sacred character of the number seven; hence, also, the original institution of the Sabbath-day. What its character was in an earlier period, chapter 4 of II Kings indicates. There the woman who asks of her husband to send her one of the young men and one of the asses, in order to visit Elisha, is reproved for her desire to go to the man of God, because " it is neither new moon nor Sabbath." The Sabbath-day at that time seems to have been a day for making excursions of the kind here described. In Deuteronomy the Sabbath is ordained as a social institution; "that thy man-servant and thy maid-servant may rest as well as thou"; is the object of its proclamation. Slaves had been the Israelites in Egypt. The slave has no rest. Israel, mindful of its own past, should afford laboring people a life worthy of men, free from the disgrace and the outrage of thraldom. The theological reason adduced in the decalogue of Exodus is the production of a much later age. There the Sabbath is ordained because God rested after His creation. No want of the human soul, no necessity of man is its root. Its object is to be a sign between God and Israel, as a later passage amplifies the fourth commandment, Exodus 31, 12-18. In the controversies on the Sabbath question in the Jewish camps, a caricature of this assumption on the part of the biblical author has often been hurled against us. It has in all seriousness been argued that man needed not the Sabbath; and unless God instituted it and we observed it for religious motives, the Sabbath-day had no function and brought no blessings to man. The example of the Greeks and Romans with disingenuous scholarship was cited in proof of the proposition. Had they not been as strong as all other races, had they not been as cultured as all others, had they not been successful in the arts, victorious in the wars, had they not speculated on the deepest themes of philosophy, and all this without having a Sabbath? The men who thus reason forget that Rome and Greece were founded on slavery. The men of leisure need indeed no Sabbath, and have no right to it. Work is one term of the Sabbath equation, rest is the other. Both terms are essential. Both are B'rith, (Aboth, R. Nathan). The avidity with which the lower classes of Rome in the centuries of her despair and decline, embraced the Sabbath institution, so that Josephus could say that there was no city, either Greek or barbarian, whither the custom of the seventh day of rest had not come (contra Apion. II, 39), and that Seneca uttered bitter complaint bewailing the imitation of the Jewish custom of the Sabbath, that Horace and Juvenal hurled the sharpest arrows of their sarcastic contempt against the Sabbath-observing Jew and Roman, plainly shows how weak the argument is, how sore its need among the working Romans.

I cannot suppress my surprise at the fact that the men, (and great Theologians are they) who conjured from the ruins Grece, the slave house of outward beauty, and Rome, whose legions carried selfishness raised to a political principle, from the laughing Adriatic to the mist-curtained German Ocean, and tyranny from the banks of the Tiber to the sands of the Lybian desert, to prove the superfluity of the Sabbath unless it be for God, should be blinded by their zeal to the blasphemy their position breathes. According to them, not the love for his children, but mere whim and caprice prompted the deity when hallowing the seventh day. The God that Judaism teaches, is not such. If He instituted the day of rest, it was not for Himself that He enacted its observance; He desired to benefit His children —the sons of man, and whatever blessings are wrapt in the institution, they may be found whatever the day of the week on which its welcome visit is expected. In Talmudical times the Sabbath became burdened with many legal restrictions. But nevertheless it remained a day of joy. Joy is the *Leitmotif* in its varied songs for the Jew. The day for him never, even under the Atlas of prohibitions superimposed by the Rabbis, was a prison-house. It was the day of human freedom. For the saying of the New Testament, "the Sabbath was made for man, and not man for the Sabbath" is an echo of a well-known Rabbinical phrase. As such a day for man, the Jewish Sabbath was equally far removed from the gloom of the Puritan caricature of the Biblical day of rest, as it was from the boisterous day of revelry and debauchery that some of the fanatics of what is falsely called "Personal Freedom," would have tolerated as the very cornerstone of human rights. Opposed as these two extremes are, they meet in this one point : they both would on Sabbath unman, man. The Puritan sets the day aside to ponder and brood over the fall of man and its consequences: he kindles the fires of hell, but not the beaming Sabbath lamp. The besotted extremist, in the other camp, would brutalise on the day man; he lights the ungodly fire of lust. The Jew has read the intention of the day. Who knows but that to its faithful observance he owes his unparalelled power of resistance to persecution, hatred, hunger, sword and pestilence?

The Sabbath, as a joyful day of rest, should first benefit the body. Life is a great usurer. It watches most scrupulously the accounts of its depositors. It will allow no overdrafts, unless repaid most amply by compounded interests on the advances. Woe to him who has fallen into the hands of this most grasping of all creditors ! Life stands upon the bond, it is inexorable. Now every stroke of the hammer on the anvil, every line of the pen, every thought flowering in the mind is paid for in the currency of blood. Blood nurtures the muscles, feeds the brain and builds the nerves. It is the balance that must always be to our credit on the ledger of life; for every outlay not replaced by a fresh deposit will visit dire consequences on him that is neglectful. And life now is still more grasping and exhausting than ever it was before.

The praises of modern culture and its great accomplishments have been sung in every key. The story of the decisive victory over nature's minions is on every canvas. The very pigments on the painter's palette are alive with power and pride, when his brush would reproduce the rush and the roar, the glow and glare, the whir and whirl of the gigantic modern work-shop. The fires beam upon us; the anvils clink; the molten iron hisses and heaves as it plunges through the rills of sand, in quest of a new guise. In the lurid light, the half shaded figures of the workers come and go, their brawny arms bared, their soot-begrimed faces eager, their eye steadily set on the task before them. Vulcan risen from the bowels of the earth—but not he with lamed foot as the ancient's fancy fashioned him. To-day his heels are spurred with Mercury's wings; the heavy pincers he carries impede not his flight. But is this glorious idealisation of the modern spirit of mechanical inventiveness and skill, and boldness, a true mirror of the realities of every-day life? Candor compels the answer: it is not. No such joy is mingled with the rattle and jingle of the real foundry. Over it hangs a cloud. The price of progress is always human blood. Not only to him who ventures first of human souls, to learn a new secret, into the hidden chambers of nature's storehouse, comes death at the threshold; not only he who hitches to the chariot of advancing humanity a new force often expires e'er the turbulent steed submits to the taming hand; but many that follow pay dearly for their curiosity or their daring. Nature brooks unwillingly the yoke; she is a treacherous slave, hating the masters' hand ever on the look-out to do him harm. She thirsteth for revenge. One moment of relaxed watchfulness commits to her pleasure life and limb of her jailer. A sudden crash, to splinters are shattered the stoutest bars, the strongest bolts of her prison house. But such moments are not many; therefore, with greater malice, with more insidious weapons, she wages the war of destruction under the mask of assumed resignation and submission. She hampers and hinders, harrasses and harms the captor wherever and whenever she may. Visit the vast halls of our industrial establishments! The air teems with small invisible particles; every inhalation deposits into the lungs vegetable or animal fibres, or metallic dust. Poisonous vapors impregnate the atmosphere, boding no good to him who is called to tarry long in these surroundings. Even where law and humanity join hands to provide the amplest and best devises to assure a new supply of air, the danger is not altogether robbed of its sharp arrow. Nature built in every human body five delicate gateways for the communication of the mind with the outer world. Up to them flows constantly the tide of impressions; and when not well shielded irreparable injury is done. Not with impunity did we steal the lightning's flash. The glare wearies the eye and dulls it. The cataract of noise that engine and hammer, wheel and needle, vie with each other to produce, soon destroys the finer sensitiveness of the ear. And furthermore the work imposed demands a certain position unrelieved for hours and hours. In consequence certain muscles are abnormally developed, while others shrivel and shrink. The spine curves, the chest narrows; the symmetry of the body is broken; the natural current of the blood impeded. Modern medicine catalogues a number of degenerations, deformities and abnormal enlargements which are directly due to the necessities of our industrial system. Almost every profession and every occupation brings in its wake certain ailments peculiar to it. The well-wisher of humanity is thus confronted with a most serious problem.

These deliterious influences must be counteracted; the avenues to health must be reopened. But how? The spells of sleep between the stretches of waking and wasting work are not sufficient for complete restoration. The blood burned is not refreshed enough, and not as large a stock of new fuel as is needed, is laid in by the nightly visit to the land of dreams. Too soon the jar and the jostle, the din and the tumult of street and factory resume their deafening rivalry. The nerves half rebuilt, the brain half replenished by the night's silence and sleep, are too soon restrung to a high pitch and strain. Every recurrent day weakens the power of the senses to transmit correct impressions from without and of the central organ to receive them, and to act upon them by directing and adjusting the execution of volition from within. A pause of longer duration is needed, and of periodic regularity, to refill the treasure-house of life energy. Physicians are of one opinion on this score. The lungs irritated during the whole week, the tubes clogged with the soot and the fibres of the shop, the blood tainted with poisons and thinned, the body twisted out of shape over the desk or at the bench: they all cry out for a whole day of freedom from exposure and outrage. A whole day to expel the injurious accumulations of the week, or to stretch again into position the spine, to give the cramped chest the liberty to expand, and the pressed liver to act normally. The day of rest is the only prophylactic against the deterioration of the race through unchecked progression of the abnormities or the deformities that to-day lurk under every boiler, and threaten not only the wage-worker, but also the merchant and the scholar.

But with a freer movement of lung and a fuller flow of rewarmed blood, comes to man the desire for activity. For the animal, rest is cessation from exercise. Man not being an animal, cannot rest inactively. Rest for man must become recreation. It means change of activity and change of surroundings. The Sabbath cannot be spent in idleness. Idleness is as great a weight upon man as is over-exertion. From idleness comes *ennui*, the source of all mischief, the root of all sin. Even on the day of rest, man needs an occupation, craves one, but that occupation must be different from the attention and activity of the week. For this reason the day of rest is intended, by nature and by God, for the cultivation of the higher things and the higher possessions of man. Man has not merely a body, he has a mind. The whir and whirl of the week days' work gives to but the chosen few the time to even catch a faint glimpse through the cracks of the door of the splendor of the palace chamber of thought. The burdens of the daily work are so great that, when with the nightfall it is lifted, the mind has not the elasticity to seek admission to the audience hall of knowledge. But with a full freedom of the day of rest the mind demands its rights. To spend a large portion of the weekly day of freedom in the cultivation of our mind is not sinful. On the contrary, it is but following the hints worked into the very fibre of our nature. Change of occupation includes change of interests. When the eye has been riveted on a bright surface for a long time, the glare becomes intolerable and painful. The organ hungers for relief. It is not advisable to drop the lids and shut out all rays; this involves an effort, and the pressure is moreover not relaxed. Before the closed eye will flit and dance sparks due to the continued nerve action. But turn in such moments of fatigue away from the flaming lines, and fix your gaze on darker grounds, the sensation of pain will immediately be soothed into that of grateful pleasure. In the same manner the mind that during the week was intensely active or concentrated on one thing, cannot at once, without injury, pass from one pole of cerebral excitement to the other pole of total torpidity. Were the attempt made the chain of ideas would roll on as if wound on a self-uncoiling bobin. Change of activity diversion of attention to a new field is the proper relief to apply. The bookish man had better hitch his thoughts to the donkey cart of the practical things of life, while the man of the desk and the cobbler at the bench turn to regions whither, neither the figures of Ledger nor the measures of the foot can follow. The Sunday newspaper is now—this cannot be gainsaid—the sole means of mental diversion for the preponder-ating majority of our people. Against this beneficial agent a crusade is preached in our midst. I, for one, fail to understand the zeal of the aggres-sive party. The work on the Sunday issue is done almost entirely before the Sabbath begins. The movement can thus not be prompted by a desire to insure a day of rest to the staff of the paper; this would lead to the suspension of Monday's issue. The old distinction between sacred things and the things secular is the moving spirit of the protest. It is an after-glow of the old Calvinistic theology. This world is under the curse of sin; its affairs are secondary to the eternalities of God's kingdom. From that kingdom man is excluded; his thought should be wrapt in the scheme of salvation. But life is stronger than dogma. The realities of hunger of ambition and their retinue knock at the gate; they must be admitted. The week is turned over to their sway; but with heavy heart should this con-cession to the sinful flesh ;be made! No smile must illumine this vale of tears; no pleasure, however innocent, be indulged in. The gloom of sin must not be forgotten. And especially on the Lord's day must no thought of worldliness be given audience. Six days' slavery to the devil: one day exclusively for God! The drudgery of work must be replaced by the dreariness of worship. The Puritanical Sabbath is the outgrowth of Calvinic theology—not a copy of the Sabbath of the Talmud. If visits to the circus, the theatre, are discountenanced by our good doctors of the Greek age, their motive was the desire to keep from moral contamination their people's heart. The shadow of the destruction of Jerusalem hovers over the horizon and tempers the joy of the Rabbis who lived during and right after the catastrophe. But the Sabbath was directly exempt from whatever restrictions the sad recollections may have placed upon the ebulition of gladness on other days. Work was indeed prohibited, but never art (CHOKMAH). They would never have dreamt of suppressing the reading of a newspaper. Of course, the Sunday paper is busy with the affairs of this world. But this alone does not enlist it into the army of corruption. For thousands and thousands it is' the only messenger of the higher intellectuality that is within their reach. It·brings to ·them not merely the news of the day, circling for them the globe; but it opens to them the life of other climes, countries and classes, and thus awakens the slumbering consciousness of the fundamental unity of all hidden under the galling differences on the surface. It discourses m a popular style on the problems of the sciences, and photographs the advance of discovery and invention. It discusses the questions of morality, both applied and pure; it is a library in itself, an epitome of current knowledge; it is an educator. If now it be said that the paper of the day is not true to its mission, the objection weighs, if true, as heavily against the week day issue. Bad is bad on Sunday as on Monday. The sensational gossiper is as intolerable on Wednesday as he is on the " Lord's day." The shortcoming of the press have been exaggerated, the good it works steadily minimised. Take our Sunday issues all in all; they are a powerful instrument wielded for the raising of the mental level of the masses.

The opening·of the reading-room of the Public Libray shocked at first the sensibilities of some and roused a storm of objections. Yet I doubt whether there be those to-day among us who would undo the measure. To visit under Tyndal's guidance the Alps, and learn from his lips the history of their birth and growth; to read the rocks with Lyell, and to watch the worm with Darwin; to study the republic of the ants with Lubbock, and with Proctor the sun; to cross with Stanley the dark continent; to sound the depth of the ocean with the crew of the " Challenger"; is a pleasure that few can seek in the brief hours after the daily task is done. Is this sinful? Is Longfellow or Whittier not an unmitred priest at the altar of truth? Is it wrong to laugh at the follies of men in this vanity fair-life, and be warned by the pointed pen of Thackeray? Is Ruth alone typical of womanly love? Are not Enid, and Maud, the miller's daughter, Lady Clare, worthy sisters of hers in the gallery and gallaxy of true and pure womanhood? Are Lowell and Browning less inspiring than are the books of Kings or the Revelation of St. John? Emerson and Elliot, and Robert Elsmere not good Sunday reading? The answer is easily found; it cannot but be in the affirmative.

How many have the time to worship at the shrine of Art, or care for its message while the wheels are spinning round and the belts are tightened? The truly beautiful is always a reflection of the truly good. The picture gallery is a church to-day, as formerly the church was a picture gallery. None who feels for and with the people can but congratulate the management of our promising Art-Institute upon the step, resolved upon by them, to open on Sunday afternoon the doors of their collection. Reggio and Rembrandt, Angelo and Murillo, Raphael and Titian, Cornelius and Kaul-

bach, cannot preach a low view of duty. Fanaticism which would hush the
sermon breathed upon the canvas overshoots the mark. The twin-sisters of
painting and sculpture, Music and Drama, will also find a hearing on the day
of rest. Music of a debased and debasing kind, is always baneful. It derides
its own parentage. But a symphony by Beethoven and Brahms, a sonata by
Mozart, an oratorio by Mendelssohn and Hayden, or Hændl; a chorus from
Parcival, a powerful overture by Meyerbeer, and even the lighter children
of melody if pure and chaste, chime as harmoniously in with the spirit of
the day as does a *Te Deum* by Palæstra or a Mass by Verdi. The stage,
decried as the arch-enemy of the church, is a potent ally. The piece that
panders to the sensual and the brutal in man is objectionable on any day.
So is also on Sunday the pulpit that caters to sensationalism. As the
Germans call it, the stage are the boards that signify the world. That is
its mission. Shakspeare, Schiller, Goethe, and all that portray the eternal
conflicts of the human heart and the contrasts of the human life, are the
most efficient aids to the preacher in his endeavors to lift man above himself. It has been said that the stage pictures vice. Perhaps it does, but it
does not glorify it. Where even the fallen are conjured from their glitter-
ing palace of shame, through them quivers the appeal of a humanity that
recognises the sister, even when burdened with sin, and warns not to judge
lest we be judged. Goodness, from an æsthetic point of view, may be
lacking in interest. "Faust is not good, Mephistopheles is candidly exe-
crable," Macbeth is a murderer. But what of that? Do we not read in
these characters the enigma of our own life? Through the true drama
runs the sentiment:

> "There's a divinity that shapes our ends.
> Rough-hew them how we will."

Such conviction cannot bring harm to a people, though it be taught on
Sunday. If, of course, beauty and recreation are in themselves sinful, if man
is depraved, if nature is under the curse of sin, if the Sunday have no other
object than to be a constant memento of man's sinfulness, all these agencies
which correspond to a natural want of man, are out of harmony with the
purposes of the day of rest. But human nature cannot be artificially
outraged, it will assert its rights, and unless these rights are legitimately
conceded, their satisfaction is sought in illegitimate direction. Close your
libraries, close your art rooms, hush the music of the concert hall, lock the
doors that lead to the temples where the world's show and the world's
substance is acted out in types created by master minds, and you will drive
the masses into the den of vice, and instead of worshipping at the shrine of
beauty, they will bend the knee to gods of wine. Action and reaction are
always equal, and it is sometimes difficult to decide which of the two is cause
and which is effect. Our ideas have changed. It is not the foreigner that
has weakened the foundations of Puritanism. There is much in Puritanism
that demands unstinted approval and admiration. Our state and union
we much to the sturdy character, the streak of Puritanism which runs

through our people, a heritage of the fathers of Plymouth rock. But the new age has come with new ideas. Character to-day is built on the same lines as of old, but by new means, new methods. The spirit of scientific investigation opening up nature's secret to us, has given the death blow to the dogma that nature is sinful and that man is degraded. Man by birth is neither degraded, nor is he divine; but he may become divine, and he may be degraded; and those'that have the best interests of man at heart, must be careful of their words and cautious in their methods. In the conflicts of modern times, everything must be used that tends "to lift man above himself." The mind needs culture, and the day of rest is for the thousands the only day to satisfy the want. Beauty and melody are potent factors in the upbuilding of human character: therefore the day of rest is not violated by allowing these factors to play upon men, women and children.

Of course, intellectual and æsthetic culture are but stepping stones to moral culture, and the day of rest should also be sacred to the cultivation of the moral element in man. That is the special function of the church and the temple. Life distracts and life narrows. Man becomes a something in consequence of this distraction and this concentration. Division of labor has in every walk of life progressed so far that no one in his work attains completeness. Day in, day out, making the same thing over and over again, we are in danger of being reduced to a mere automaton. Under this specialization, we lose consciousness of our " man-ness." Religion comes as the preacher of the truth that man is not something, but some one, and that he as some one belongs to a larger life, is associated with others that are some one, and is kin to that life which is the all in all, and which in an attempt to describe it and bring it near unto us, we call "our God, our Father who is in heaven." For this reason religious culture, religious exercises, service and sermon are an integral part of the proper celebration of the Sabbath. The hours of the morning of the Sabbath-day should undoubtedly be devoted to religious aspirations, the afternoon may be consecrated to the other agencies of culture. It is argued that the Sunday newspaper and the other things conflict with the attendance in churches. The causes lie deeper. Let the church search, and the temple as well, her own conduct and her own methods, and all of us will perhaps discover that the evil of religious indifference is largely due to our own shortcomings. The church has become not the home of the lame and the burdened, the weak and the lowly. It is the luxury of the rich, of the chosen favored sons in the family of mankind. The jargon of church and temple alike is the dry-rot of dogmatism, not the full-blown rose of duty. What attraction lies in hearing over and over again the ancient controversies or the old disputes of scholastic dogmatists? Man to-day has outgrown the fears of childhood, and the fires of hell will not strike terror to his heart, so that driven by anguish and anxiety he should flee to the altar of God and seek there an asylum from the pursuer. Or the pulpit rivals the circus-clown! Mountebanks with shallow verbiage usurp the places where men of sound scholarship should teach. They attract, indeed, many, but disgust countless thousands more, and do more harm than short-sighted admirers will admit!

The light of religion must be thrown on the issues of the day. The whole world is God's creation. There is in the scale of Godliness nothing great and nothing small. The contrasts of modern life, the burdens of modern problems must be eased; and if this were the ambition of the preachers, no doubt is in my mind but the Sunday would again become for the thousands a welcome opportunity to visit the shrine of God. To the field of moral culture belongs also the cultivation of friendship. The day of rest is sacred to the family, is sacred to the intercourse of soul with soul. On that day father should meet son and mother meet daughter, each one looking into the eye and into the heart of the other, read of the week's accomplishments and remember the week's anxieties; and thus giving and drawing strength from the sweet covenant of love, become stronger again for the week's waiting work, and better for the week's demanding duty. Moral culture may come through the whispered fragrance of the rose and the soft waving of the foliage of the trees. In proper season to visit the parks, to recline at the breast of nature in spring time, is a profitable way of spending the day of rest. There we find "tongues in trees, books in the running brooks, sermons in stones and good in everything." How many of the children of the city, even in the faintest manner, know aught of the hidden beauties of the fields, of the music of the brooks, and of the murmuring of the lakes? Pent up in their pens and crowded and huddled together in their tenement lodgings, whither scarce ever the full ray of the sun penetrates, breathing hour after hour the heavily laden atmosphere of the workshop and the mingled vapors of their own restricted quarters, their lungs and their body need the rejuvenating elixir of hours spent in the open air in the sunshine, under the trees. If in company of their own family they will be safe from the temptations that beset him who seeks pleasure selfishly. Intercourse with nature on the Sabbath-day is not sinful, it is saintly. Remove the sting of the forbidden fruit and its charm from these innocent joys, and you need not fear that injurious pleasures will be sought. The revelry deplorable on any day and which is most noticeable on Sunday, is not a characteristic of the German. Have they who of late have wasted much eloquence in their attack on the German Sabbath-breaker, ever stopped to think why it is that in Europe and in Germany, while the Sabbath is not observed in the Puritan fashion, yet scarce ever one meets in the streets the reeling figure of a man intoxicated or hears the furious cries of one frenzied by alcoholic drink? It is because nature is open, because the family is together on that day, because what joys are sought remain joys, that is to say, innocent and not selfish; it is because public opinion has not affixed the stigma of sin to certain things that may be in their excess deplorable, but which partaken of as the true man will partake of them, are absolutely harmless. It is because love throws her armor around husband or son and keeps him from besotting himself, knowing that wife or sister would spurn him from her company were he to court the passionate embrace of fiery drinks.

What now should the state do? This let me in conclusion inquire into in regard to the observation of the Sabbath! Religion and state are happily divorced. Their marriage was always illegitimate, and if the Sabbath is observed merely on religious ground, the state ought to have no concern with it. But the state has the function to be the guardian of the community's interest, to be the protector of the weaker in the community. Selfishness is as yet, even according to the open profession of the writers on economic subjects, the sole motive of action in industrial mercantile life. The selfishness of an individual in the vast chain of mercantile exchanges, produces almost of necessity the selfishness of all others. As competition is the highest law of trade, every advantage gained by one must be striven after by all others. As things are, man as considered a factor in industrial life, has become a mere hand, a tool, a thing. Competition allows not to measure him by another standard and to treat him according to other precepts of morality. Therefore, it is the state's duty to watch that not the selfishness of the worst demand, as a consequence, the succession of the selfishness of the less bad, or even of the best. Every man should, by law, be guaranteed the enjoyment of the day of rest. Remove the Sunday laws, as far as they apply to this guarantee from our statute books, and competition will soon have effected that for six days' hire seven days work will be exacted from all. The misery of the masses under our present system will always be great enough to supply, under the higher sceptre of starvation threatened, the demand for men to work seven days at pay of six. Of course, in the long-run, better work is turned out by the hands that rest one day in seven. But what cares grasping selfishness for ulterior advantages? It is the present, immediate profit, that it craves for. Unless hindered, it will disregard humanity and future benefits for the gratification of its greed. To prevent this patent danger is the duty of the state. Further than this, and of course the maintenance and the guardianship of public peace and the prevention of interference by the one with the rights of the other, the state has no concern with the observation of the Sabbath. Education will, in the course of time, tend to give the American people a Sabbath day of uniform character. It will be what the day of rest is intended for, a day for man and by man, for the higher life of man, cultivation of the higher things of life, and the study of the higher themes of life, a day which will be free from the riot, the revelry, the boisterousness, the drunkenness of the fanatics, of what they call falsely the personal freedom to intoxicate themselves whenever they choose, and equally free from the narrowness or fanaticism of Puritan dogmatism. It will be a day whereon the church will have a wider circle of friends than now, and a deeper influence, but a day whereon art and music, authors and students will also dispense blessings.

On the morn of the day of nature's resurrection to new life, in Gœthe's *Faust*, the student from his dingy study and the narrow streets of the town, hurries through the gates, crosses the ditch and seeks the open air of the country. With him many wend their way in search after the breezes of early spring.

> *Hier ist des Volkes wahrer Himmel,*
> *Zufrieden jauchzet Gross und Klein,*
> *Hier bin ich Mensch, hier darf ich's sein.*

Hier bin ich Mensch. So comes it to him with the full tide of a new life, a new life around about him. The day of rest is in the Christian church the day of the resurrection, but as our Goethe says,

> *Sie feiern die Auferstehung des Hernn,*
> *Denn sie sind selber auferstanden.*

The day of rest, this is the truth of the Christian dogma, is the day whereon each man rises to the higher life. *Hier bin ich Mensch.* A day whereon comes to us the thought, the inspiration, the knowledge that, regardless of the contrasts of the week, free from the cares and the concerns of the week day, free and larger than its concentrations, and broader than its limitations, is the life of man. The day of rest proclaims to each one, *Hier bist Du Mensch;* now " Thou art a man, the son, the image of God."

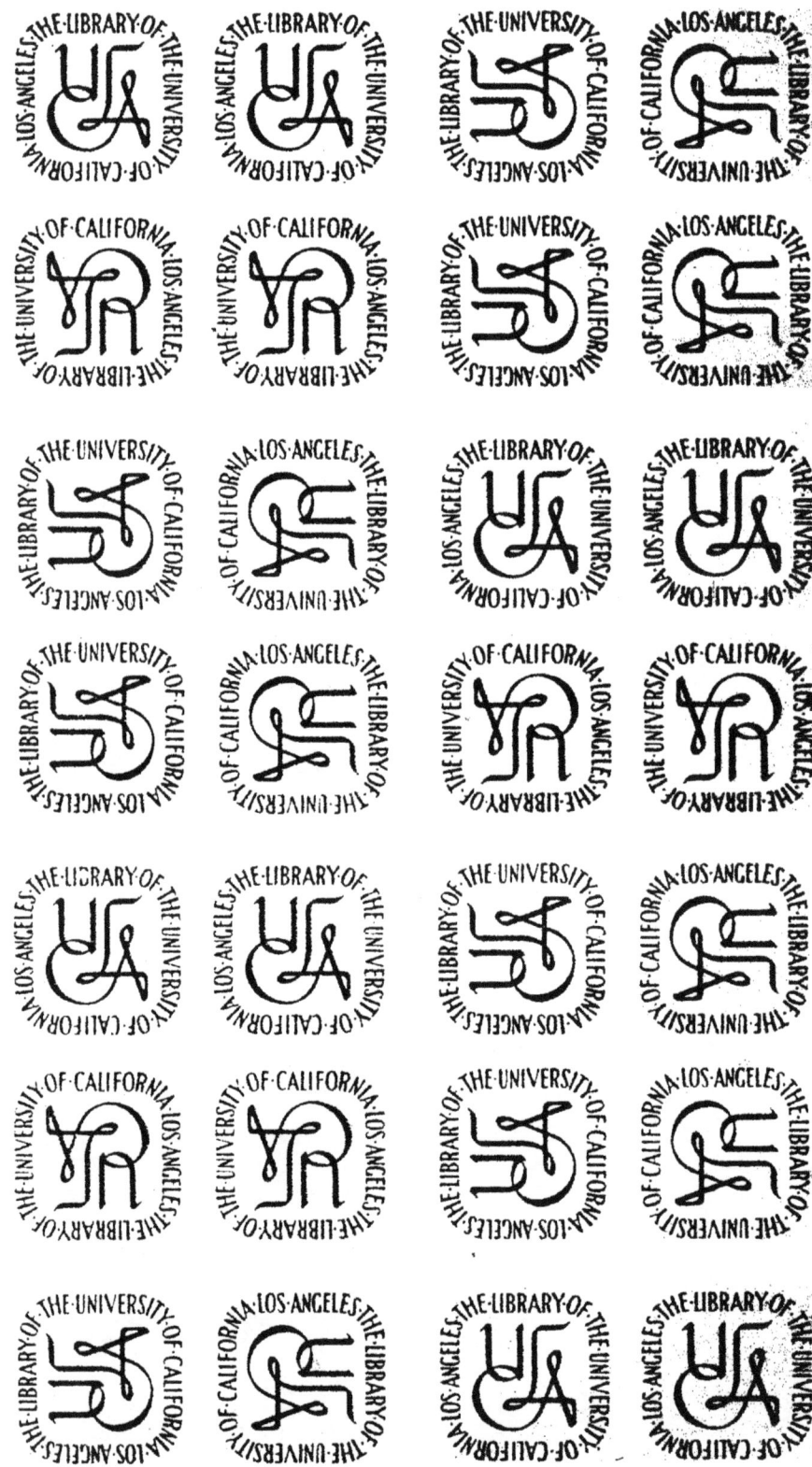